The Science of Weather

LIVING SCIENCE

Janice Parker

Gareth Stevens Publishing
A WORLD ALMANAC EDUCATION GROUP COMPANY

For a free color catalog describing Gareth Stevens' list of high-quality books and multimedia programs, call 1-800-542-2595 (USA) or 1-800-461-9120 (Canada). Gareth Stevens Publishing's Fax: (414) 225-0377.

Library of Congress Cataloging-in-Publication Data available upon request from publisher. Fax (414) 225-0377 for the attention of the Publishing Records Department.

ISBN 0-8368-2684-1 (lib. bdg.)

This edition first published in 2000 by
Gareth Stevens Publishing
A World Almanac Education Group Company
1555 North RiverCenter Drive, Suite 201
Milwaukee, WI 53212 USA

Project Co-ordinator: Rennay Craats
Series Editor: Celeste Peters
Copy Editors: Megan Lappi and Heather Kissock
Design: Warren Clark
Cover Design: Lucinda Cage and Terry Paulhus
Layout: Lucinda Cage
Gareth Stevens Editor: Patricia Lantier-Sampon

Every reasonable effort has been made to trace ownership and to obtain permission to reprint copyright material. The publishers would be pleased to have any errors or omissions brought to their attention so that they may be corrected in subsequent printings.

Photograph Credits:
Corbis: pages 25 bottom, 28. Corel Corporation: cover (background); pages 5 top, 5 bottom, 6 top, 6 bottom, 8 left, 10 top left, 10 top right, 10 bottom left, 10 bottom right, 12 far left, 12 middle right, 12 far right, 13 far left, 13 middle left, 13 middle right, 13 far right, 14, 16 left, 17 middle right, 17 bottom left, 21 right, 31. Digital Stock: cover (middle); pages 7, 15 top, 16 top right, 16 bottom right, 17 top left, 18, 19 bottom, 20, 22 top left, 23, 24, 25 top, 26, 27, 29 top left, 29 middle right, 29 bottom. EyeWire: page 30. PhotoDisc: pages 4, 5 middle right. Tom Stack & Associates: pages 15 bottom (Tom Stack), 19 top (John Shaw), 22 bottom right (Dr. Scott Norquay). Visuals Unlimited: pages 8 right (Arthur R. Hill), 12 middle left (Inga Spence), 21 left (Mark A. Schneider).

Printed in Canada

1 2 3 4 5 6 7 8 9 04 03 02 01 00

Contents

What Do You Know about Weather?

What might often seem invisible, but has a powerful role in our lives? Weather! All living things must live with weather. Weather refers to the outside environment, including sunshine, rain, snow, wind, heat, and cold. Different areas of the world have different types of weather.

Rain storms often bring flashes of lightning with them.

We often think about temperature when we think of weather. Temperature tells us how hot or cold it is outside. Temperature is measured in degrees on a **thermometer**. The number of degrees goes up as the temperature gets warmer. The lower the temperature, the colder it is outside.

In most areas on Earth, temperatures are higher in summer than in winter. Areas near the **equator** have almost the same temperature all year round.

Activity

Measuring Temperature

Measure the temperature in two different areas outdoors. Place one thermometer in the shade. Then place another thermometer in the sunshine. How different are the temperatures in the two areas?

Weather in the Air

The layer of air around Earth is called the **atmosphere**. It contains many gases. For example, the oxygen we breathe is a gas found in the atmosphere. The carbon dioxide that plants rely on is a gas in the air, too.

The atmosphere also contains small particles of dust and water. Water is a very important part of the atmosphere. Clouds and rain develop from water in the air.

When the wind blows more often from one direction, it is called a prevailing wind. This wind can make trees grow to one side.

Pieces of dust attract water in the atmosphere, creating water droplets. These droplets form clouds in the sky.

Weather is the condition of the atmosphere where we live. What is the atmosphere like today? Is it moving around, causing wind storms? Is it very still, clear, and warm? Is it filled with gray clouds that block the Sun? The condition of the atmosphere seems to change all the time. As conditions change, so does the weather.

Activity

Invisible Air

A string can show how forces we cannot always see in the atmosphere can play a role in the weather.

1. Cut a piece of string 6 inches (15.2 cm) long.
2. Blow gently on the string. Your breath moves the string by moving the air. The moving air creates an invisible breeze. To create a stronger breeze, blow harder against the string.

Sometimes the weather is violent. Hurricanes are giant storms in the atmosphere.

Sun and Wind

Of the millions of stars in the sky, the Sun is the star nearest to Earth. It acts as Earth's furnace. Energy from the Sun travels to Earth and heats the air, ground, and water. During the day, the ground becomes warmer than the air and water. The warm ground then heats the air above it at night.

A weather vane shows which direction the wind is blowing.

Scientists estimate the Sun's inner temperature at 25,000,000° F (14,000,000° C).

Winds are movements of the air caused by differences in air temperature. Warm air rises. Colder air rushes underneath the warm air. This creates wind in the atmosphere. Without wind, the weather would change very little from one day to the next.

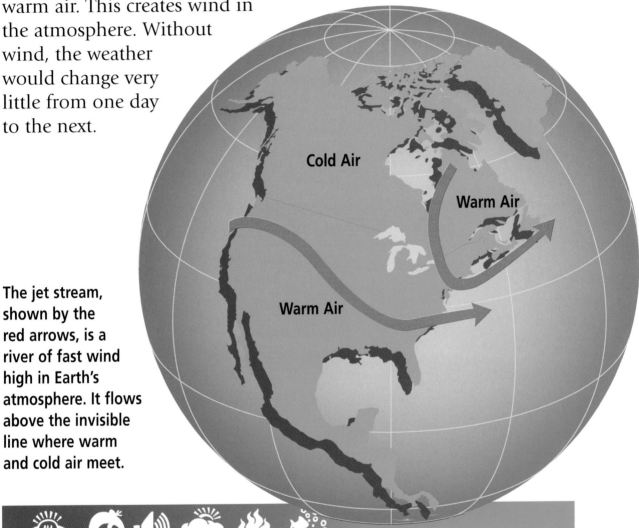

Cold Air

Warm Air

Warm Air

The jet stream, shown by the red arrows, is a river of fast wind high in Earth's atmosphere. It flows above the invisible line where warm and cold air meet.

Puzzler

How can you tell which direction the wind is blowing if you do not have a weather vane?

Answer:
Look for a tree or bush that is bent over by the wind. It is bent in the direction the wind is blowing. Or, lick one side of your finger, hold it up, and turn it around. The wet side will feel coldest when it is facing the direction from which the wind is blowing.

The Seasons

Changes in weather are often seen as different seasons. In winter, the Sun remains low in the sky. Winter days are the shortest and coldest of the year. In summer, the Sun rises high in the sky. Summer days are the longest and hottest of the year.

autumn

winter

In spring, trees begin to bloom. By summer, tree branches are heavy with leaves and flowers. As autumn approaches, the leaves start to change color and fall off the branches. Trees are bare by the time winter arrives.

summer

spring

In most areas of the world, each year is divided into four seasons. The seasons are spring, summer, autumn, and winter. Earth circles the Sun once a year, and it tilts at an angle toward or away from the Sun. This causes the seasons. During summer, Earth tilts toward the Sun. In winter, it tilts away from the Sun.

Earth's path around the Sun causes seasons to occur at the same time each year. The illustration below shows a side view of Earth, illustrating the seasons for the northern hemisphere. The seasons are opposite for the southern hemisphere.

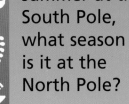

Puzzler

When it is summer at the South Pole, what season is it at the North Pole?

Answer:
Winter

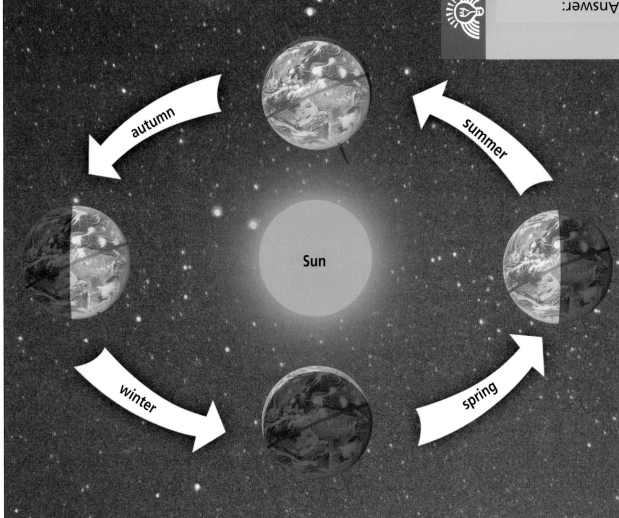

autumn

summer

Sun

winter

spring

Climates around the World

Every area of the world has its own weather patterns. For example, areas close to the equator have the same weather all year. In other areas of the world, some parts of the year are wetter or warmer than others. These different regional weather patterns are called **climates**.

Types of Climates

Tropical Rain Forest	Monsoon	Grassland	Desert

• close to the equator • very hot and wet every day	• found north and south of tropical rain forests • two seasons — a hot, wet summer and a cool, dry winter	• large, flat, grassy areas • little rain most of the year • some showers in summer	• found on every continent • very dry, sometimes no rain for years

Examples

African rain forests, Amazon rain forests	India, West Africa	Great Plains, Serengeti Plains	Mojave Desert, Sahara Desert

Puzzler

Where might be the best place to live if cold, wet weather makes your joints ache?

Answer:
Many people who suffer from aching joints choose to live in or near the desert, where it is warm and dry all year.

Temperate	Boreal Forest	Mountain	Polar

• halfway between the equator and the poles • hot summers, cool to cold winters	• northern forest areas • cold, dry, long winters and warm, showery summers	• mountain areas • warm days, cool or cold nights • often windy	• near the North and South poles • long, dark, very cold winters and cold, sunny summers
most of North America and Europe	northern forests in Canada and Russia	Rocky Mountains, European Alps	Greenland, Iceland

Water, Water Everywhere

The air around us contains a large amount of water. Most water droplets in the air are so tiny we cannot see them. These droplets are called **water vapor**.

Water vapor comes from oceans, lakes, ponds, and puddles. Water at the surface **evaporates**, or turns into vapor. The air then absorbs, or takes in, this vapor. Warm air absorbs more water vapor than cool air.

Air cools during the night. Water vapor settles onto plants as dew.

Clouds form when warm air rises in the atmosphere. As the air gets higher, it becomes colder. Because cold air cannot hold as much water as warm air, the water vapor **condenses** at this point and forms drops of water. When this happens, clouds become visible.

Moisture from oceans rises to form clouds.

On cold, winter days you can see your breath in the air. Your warm breath hits the cold air, and the water vapor condenses.

Activity

Vapor Caper

Water is disappearing! Pretend you are a detective and discover where it is going.

1. With an adult's help, boil water on a stove. As the water boils, it turns into steam.
2. Watch the steam rise. See it vanish into thin air? It turns into invisible water vapor absorbed by the air!
3. You can prove the water has gone into the air. Ask an adult to put on an oven mitt. Steam is very hot and can burn you. Now ask your helper to hold a cold pot lid high over the steam. What happens? Do you see water droplets condensing on the lid?

Cloud Types

Clouds have different names depending on their shape and how high they are in the sky. They can sit many miles up in the air or low near the ground.

Stratus Clouds
are low and flat. They cover the sky like a ceiling.

Cirrus Clouds
are small and wispy. They appear high in the sky, usually during cold weather.

Cumulus Clouds
are fluffy and white. They change shape constantly. They are usually in the sky on warm, sunny days.

Cumulonimbus Clouds

appear during thunderstorms.
They are tall and dark.

Fog

is a cloud that is low to the ground.
It is often very difficult to see through fog.

Mist

is not as thick as fog.
It lies very close to the ground.

Activity

Keep a Cloud Journal

Look in the sky for clouds every day. Describe the amount, shape, and color of the clouds. Also write down what the weather is like that day. Which clouds come with what sort of weather?

Rain and Snow

Rain and snow are forms of **precipitation**. Precipitation is water that falls from clouds to the ground. Moisture from seas and oceans rises into the air and forms clouds. In the tropics, rain begins as tiny water droplets in the clouds. These droplets join together to form larger droplets. When these are heavy enough, they fall to the ground as rain.

Too much rain can destroy communities. If more water falls than the soil or rivers can contain, the area **floods**.

In temperate areas of Earth, moisture in clouds falls as snow. In summer, the snow drops through warm layers of air and melts to fall as rain. If the rain then drops through a layer of cold air, it freezes into sleet. Hail forms when strong winds carry ice crystals up and down through cold, moist air. The moisture freezes to the ice crystals, making them grow large enough to fall to Earth.

No two snowflakes are exactly the same.

Puzzler

How much water does snow make?

Answer: Snow is very light and airy. If you melt 10 inches (25.4 cm) of snow, you will get only 1 inch (2.54 cm) of water.

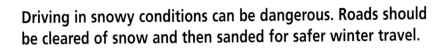
Driving in snowy conditions can be dangerous. Roads should be cleared of snow and then sanded for safer winter travel.

Thunder and Lightning

Thunderstorms are very powerful. During thunderstorms, electricity in the clouds creates lightning. A lightning flash heats the air around it. The air explodes, and we hear the crashing sound of thunder.

Lightning heats the air around it to 60,000° F (33,000° C) when it strikes.

We see lightning as soon as it happens. Light moves very quickly. It travels 186,282 miles (299,727 kilometers) per second. Sound does not travel as quickly. It takes five seconds to travel one mile (1.6 km). This is why we hear thunder after we see lightning.

A flash of lightning can cause fires and damage. Trees can be split in half by a lightning strike.

Thunderhead clouds let us know a storm is coming.

Puzzler

How can you tell the distance between yourself and a lightning strike?

Answer:
Count the seconds between seeing the flash and hearing the boom. Divide the number of seconds by five. This tells you how many miles away the lightning was. For example, if you count 10 seconds, the lightning was 2 miles (3.2 km) away.

Blowing in Circles

Tornadoes are spinning **funnels** of air that come from the bottom of thunderclouds. Their winds can blow at speeds of more than 300 miles (480 kilometers) per hour. Most tornadoes last about half an hour. They can do great damage if they touch buildings or other objects on the ground.

Tornadoes are also called twisters.

Waterspouts are tornadoes that form over water.

Hurricanes are storms that form over the ocean in warm climates. They bring heavy rain and strong winds. Their winds can tear up trees and destroy buildings. Hurricanes can also force huge amounts of ocean water to come on land. When this happens, people near the coast are in danger of drowning.

Scientists can tell when a hurricane is coming. Many people leave the area before the storm arrives.

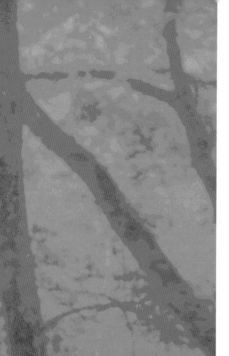

Weather and People

Weather can change the way people feel. Sunny, warm weather often puts people in good moods. Some people are depressed when the weather turns cold and cloudy. Others enjoy colder weather. People who like winter sports are happy when a lot of snow falls.

Snowstorms can prevent people from going to work or school.

Farmers depend on the weather to grow food. Their crops need sunshine and warmth. They also need rainy days after dry weather. In some areas of the world, the land is so dry that crops cannot survive.

Crops need just the right amount of rain to grow well.

Activity

Dress for the Weather

Make a list of several different types of weather. Then make a list of the clothing you would wear in each weather condition. Draw a picture of yourself dressed for each type of weather. Remember to include sunscreen on a sunny day and an umbrella on a rainy day!

Sunshine on hot days can cause sunburns.

Predicting Tomorrow's Weather

It is important to know what the weather will be like over the next few days. People need time to prepare when bad weather is coming.

Clouds help us **forecast** the weather. Low, dark clouds often mean it will rain.

Scientists use weather **satellites** and **radar** to predict the weather. Weather satellites take pictures of Earth from space. The pictures show the direction winds are blowing. They also show where clouds are and how much water they contain. Satellites even measure the temperature of clouds, ground, and water.

Radar is a device that locates an object using radio waves. Radar bounces a signal off rain or snow in clouds. This helps scientists determine how fast a storm is moving and where it is going.

Activity

Forecast the Weather

Can you predict what the weather will be tomorrow?

1. Look at the sky today. Are there any clouds? What kind of clouds are they?
2. Is the wind blowing? Look at the clouds. Note which direction the wind is pushing them.
3. Measure the temperature.
4. Now guess what the temperature and weather will be tomorrow. Perhaps your cloud journal can help. See if your predictions come true.

Satellite pictures help predict the weather several days ahead.

Meteorologists Have a Predictable Career

Meteorologists are people who predict the weather. They use satellite pictures and radar to watch weather patterns. Meteorologists understand the signs of bad weather. They warn people of dangerous weather in the area.

Meteorologists build and maintain weather stations all over the world, including the Antarctic.

Meteorologists usually have a degree from a college or university. Some meteorologists work for the government. Others provide weather forecasts over the radio or television.

Complicated maps help meteorologists predict the weather.

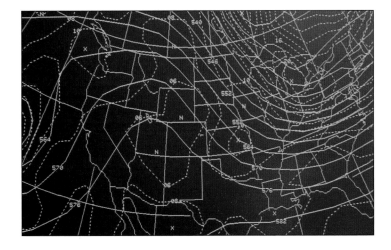

Meteorologists use the latest technology to make accurate weather forecasts.

Activity

Do Your Own Research

Many careers are related to the weather. Have a parent or teacher help you learn more about one of the following careers:

- clothing designer
- emergency services planner
- radar technician

- snowplow operator
- storm chaser
- television weather forecaster

Weather and Pollution

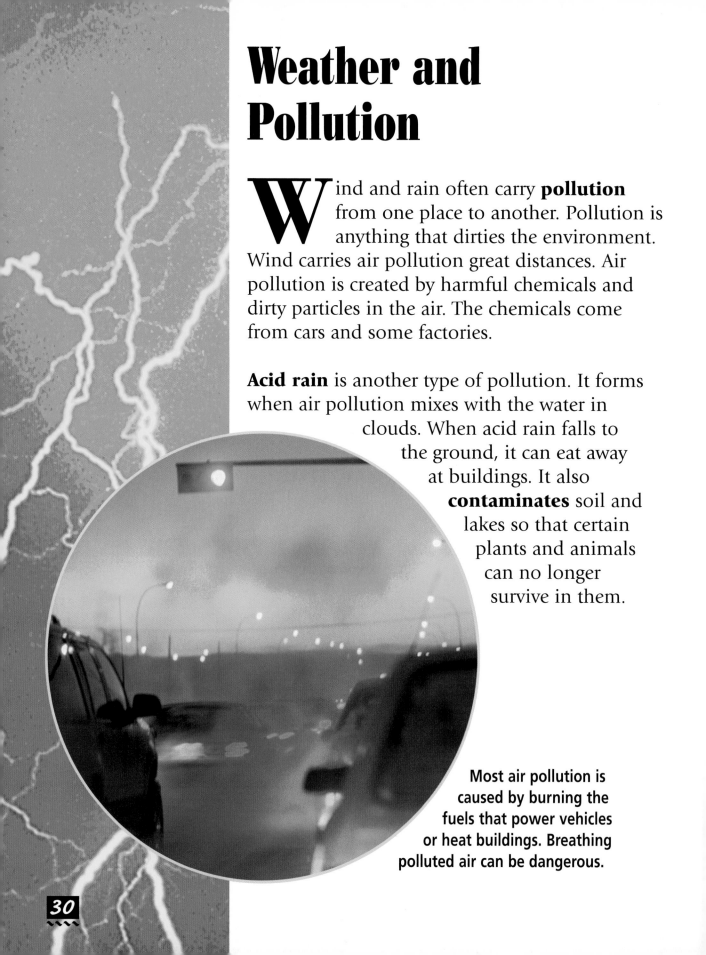

Wind and rain often carry **pollution** from one place to another. Pollution is anything that dirties the environment. Wind carries air pollution great distances. Air pollution is created by harmful chemicals and dirty particles in the air. The chemicals come from cars and some factories.

Acid rain is another type of pollution. It forms when air pollution mixes with the water in clouds. When acid rain falls to the ground, it can eat away at buildings. It also **contaminates** soil and lakes so that certain plants and animals can no longer survive in them.

Most air pollution is caused by burning the fuels that power vehicles or heat buildings. Breathing polluted air can be dangerous.

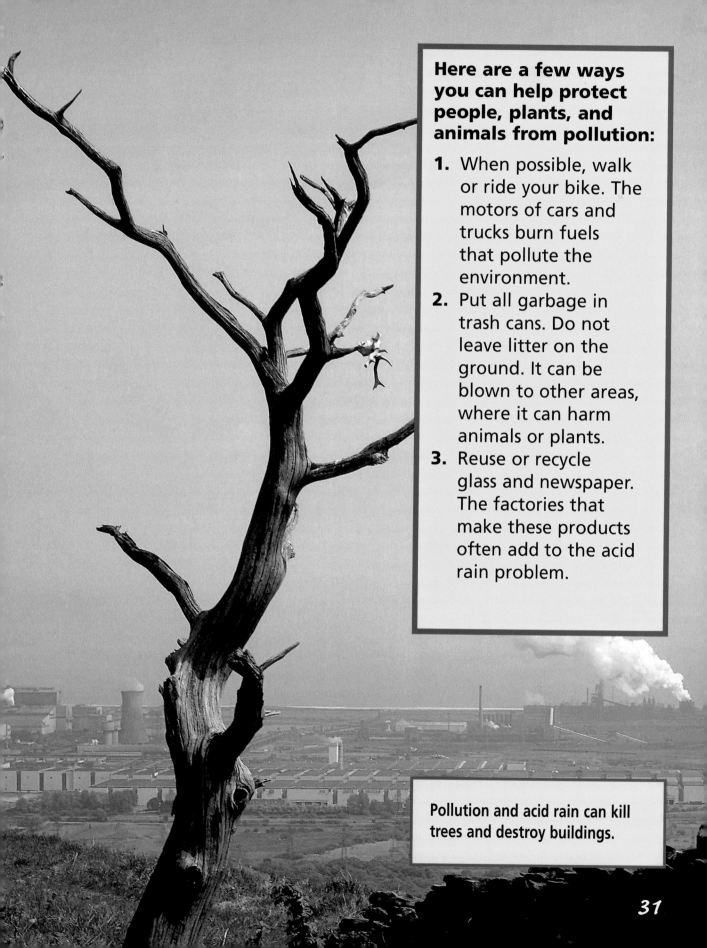

Here are a few ways you can help protect people, plants, and animals from pollution:

1. When possible, walk or ride your bike. The motors of cars and trucks burn fuels that pollute the environment.
2. Put all garbage in trash cans. Do not leave litter on the ground. It can be blown to other areas, where it can harm animals or plants.
3. Reuse or recycle glass and newspaper. The factories that make these products often add to the acid rain problem.

Pollution and acid rain can kill trees and destroy buildings.

Glossary

acid rain: rain that contains chemicals from air pollution.
atmosphere: the blanket of air that surrounds Earth.
climate: the general weather conditions of a region.
condense: come more closely together.
contaminate: to make dirty or impure; to poison.
equator: the imaginary line around Earth's middle that separates it into the northern and southern hemispheres.

evaporates: turns into vapor.
floods: too much rain or melted snow causing rivers to overflow into surrounding land areas.
forecast: a prediction of what weather will be like during the next few days.
funnel: a circular object that is wide at the top and narrow at the bottom.
meteorologist: a person trained in the science of weather, atmosphere, and climate.

pollution: harmful chemicals in the environment.
precipitation: water or snow that falls to Earth from clouds.
radar: a device that uses radio waves to locate certain objects.
satellite: an object in space that circles Earth.
thermometer: a device that measures temperature.
water vapor: tiny droplets of water in the air.

Index

Web Sites

Some web sites stay current longer than others. For further web sites, use your search engines to locate the following topics: *forecasting, hurricanes, tornadoes, snow,* and *weather satellites.*